RICHMOND
IN OLD PHOTOGRAPHS

RICHMOND BRIDGE, early twentieth century.

Front Cover Illustration:
RICHMOND BRIDGE AND RIVERSIDE (detail) by George Hilditch, C. 1855.

RICHMOND
IN OLD PHOTOGRAPHS

COMPILED BY

MEMBERS OF THE RICHMOND LOCAL HISTORY SOCIETY

EDITED BY

JOHN CLOAKE

ALAN SUTTON

Alan Sutton Publishing Limited
Phoenix Mill · Far Thrupp · Stroud · Gloucestershire

First published 1990

British Library Cataloguing in Publication Data

Richmond in old photographs
1. London. Richmond upon Thames (London Borough), history
I. Cloake, John   II. Richmond Local History Society
942.195

ISBN 0-86299-855-7

The members of the Richmond Local History Society who have co-operated in
compiling this book are:
Heather and Thomas Beagley, John Cloake, John Moses and John Plant

Typeset in 9/10 Korinna.
Typesetting and origination by
Alan Sutton Publishing.
Printed in Great Britain by
Dotesios Printers Limited.

CONTENTS

RICHMOND BREWERY AND BOATHOUSES. Calotype by Fox Talbot, c. 1840. (Courtesy of the Trustees of the Science Museum)

INTRODUCTION

'The King, having finished much of his new building at his manor of Shene and again furnished and repaired that before was perished with fire ... [commanded] that from then forth it should be named his manor of Richmond, and not Shene.'

Thus the chronicler of London recorded Henry VII's renaming of his royal palace and manor in 1501; the village of Shene promptly adopted the new name. King Henry's was the third palace on the site by the river. Edward III had first converted the manor house into a palace. Henry V and VI had rebuilt it. There were to be four more royal palaces at Richmond and Kew after the destruction of Henry VII's in the 1650s.

A book of *Richmond in Old Photographs* cannot show more than the one, modest, survivor at Kew of these palaces – and a glimpse of a remaining part of the Tudor one. 'Richmond' we have interpreted as the old Borough of Richmond as it existed before the local government changes of 1965 – including Kew and North Sheen, and the villages of Petersham and Ham – but we have stretched the boundaries to cover all of Richmond Park. We cannot, however, stretch the period

RICHMOND RIVERSIDE by George Hilditch, c. 1855.

covered by photographs beyond a century and a half. Nevertheless, Richmond's earlier history has importance for the appreciation of the nineteenth- and early twentieth-century views presented here. Because of its royal connections and because of its location – its hill and its river – Richmond grew from a village to a fashionable and flourishing small town long before the railway brought it into the London suburbs.

Because the Tudor court spent much time at Richmond, courtiers and noblemen bought, built or rented houses there. In the sixteenth century Kew developed from a tiny hamlet to become the home of great potentates. In the late seventeenth and eighteenth centuries the nobility also colonized Petersham and Ham.

The area was close to London – only two or three hours by horse, coach or river – and was renowned for its clean air and its pleasant situation. The courtiers were followed by the rich and the fashionable. From the 1690s onwards there was much speculative building in Richmond to satisfy the demand for houses for the summer use of rich Londoners. (In the early eighteenth century practically every rich Jewish merchant of London had a summer home in Richmond.) Throughout that century, new 'stately homes' sprang up along the riverside and on the Hill, and on the roads leading into the town.

Richmond was not a market town, but a resort. The summer population required entertainment. A medicinal spring was developed in the 1690s as

RICHMOND BRIDGE by George Hilditch, 1856.

Richmond Wells and enjoyed half-a-century of fashionable favour. There were regular concerts and balls. Theatres were built. New hotels and assembly rooms developed from some of the old inns and taverns. Leading figures in the arts and literature came to join the Richmond scene. Countless artists painted the beautiful Richmond Bridge and the splendid view from Richmond Hill.

Then in 1846 came the railway, which made access to London much easier and cheaper. Richmond expanded rapidly as a suburb. The fields on the slopes of the Hill were the first to be covered with villas for the middle class moving out of the capital. When a new line was opened through Kew to Hammersmith and a station built near Kew Gardens the fields between Richmond and Kew were also quickly filled with houses. Petersham escaped major development; Ham also, until the second half of the twentieth century.

The railway traffic was not confined to commuters. Richmond became a most popular place for a cheap day trip out of London. The riverside with its hundreds of boats for hire, Richmond Park and Kew Gardens, all provided recreation and relaxation; innumerable tea shops and tea gardens and pubs provided refreshment.

Many of the great old houses have now gone; but enough late-seventeenth- and

THE THAMES AT RICHMOND by George Hilditch, c. 1855.

eighteenth-century buildings remain, especially around Kew Gardens and Richmond Green, on Richmond Hill, in Petersham village and on Ham Common, to give a flavour of Richmond of old. Some of our photographs show how much has changed; but some show how much remains the same.

Richmond's first connection with photography was a very early one. The French pioneer, Joseph Nicéphore Niepce, was living in Kew in 1827 when his discoveries in photography were presented to the Royal Society. But if Niepce attempted any photographs of the Richmond scene, none have, alas, been traced. What is believed to be the earliest surviving photographic view of Richmond is one of the riverside taken by the English pioneer, William Henry Fox Talbot, about 1840 (see p. 6).

Some ten years later George Hilditch, a local gentleman who was an accomplished landscape painter, developed an interest in the new medium. Several of his photographs of local views survive to give us a glimpse of Richmond in the 1850s. Four are shown here in the Introduction; others are on the front cover and on pp. 53 and 54.

The greatest number of the photographs in this book date from the 1890s and the first decade of the twentieth century. Richmond was fortunate to have at that

THE DYSART ARMS, PETERSHAM by George Hilditch, 1852.

time some keen photographers whose work was deposited in the Public Library. It forms the nucleus of a splendid collection of local archive photographs, which has been the principal source of our material.

The first eight sections consist of a tour through the area, from Kew in the north to Ham and Richmond Park in the south. Sections Nine to Nineteen illustrate a number of themes of life and work in Richmond.

John Cloake
President
Richmond Local History Society

Kew
and North Sheen

Kew Gardens. Entrance Gates. W.2939

THE MAIN GATES OF KEW GARDENS, c. 1900. Formerly part of the royal estate, the Royal Botanic Gardens, Kew, have been in public ownership since 1840. The entrance gates were designed by Decimus Burton in 1848. The ironwork was made by Walker of Rotherham and the stone pillars by J. Hemming Junior. Standing in the gateway is one of the garden constables, in a uniform that was worn until the 1950s.

KEW PALACE, OR 'THE DUTCH HOUSE', c. 1900. Built for a merchant, Samuel Fortrey, in 1631, the house was rented by the royal family when they lived at Richmond Lodge and in the nearby White House. It became 'the Palace' when the White House was demolished (the sundial marks its site). The fence separating the Palace from the gardens has since been removed.

THE ORANGERY was Museum No. 3, clad in creeper and devoted to timber, at the turn of the century.

THE PAGODA, built, as was the Orangery, by Sir William Chambers in 1761, remains a symbol of Kew.

PAGODA VISTA, with the Temperate House on the right. The trees, recently planted when this photograph was taken, are now full-grown.

ERECTION OF THE THIRD FLAGSTAFF, 1919. There have been four flagstaffs at Kew since 1861, each taller than the last. All were Douglas firs from British Columbia. The present flagstaff was erected in 1949.

THE HERBARIUM, formerly Hunter House, was purchased by George IV in 1820. Since 1852 it has been the principal library and herbarium of the Gardens. New buildings have been added since 1899, the date of the photograph.

ST ANNE'S CHURCH, C. 1875, a well-known landmark on Kew Green, was originally a small chapel built in 1714 on land given by Queen Anne. None of the original building remains, for the church has been enlarged many times. Two major works of enlargement were carried out by Sir Jeffry Wyatville in 1837 (at the expense of King William IV), when the present west front was built, and – after the date of this photograph – the rebuilding of the east end by Henry Stock in 1884, when the cupola was added.

THE INTERIOR OF ST ANNE'S CHURCH, c. 1918. The south chapel of the chancel was converted into a war memorial chapel in 1920.

THE EMBROIDERED PEW CUSHIONS were made by members of the St Anne's Church Tapestry Guild. Illustrating Kew's history, they were designed – as was the whole project – by the Kew architect and historian George Cassidy; the ladies are Mrs Lily Pusey, Mrs Ursula Holtum and Mrs Marjorie Charles.

THE NORTH SIDE OF KEW GREEN, 1951. At the beginning of the seventeenth century the tiny hamlet of Kew was entirely within what is now Kew Gardens. Gradually the north and south sides of the Green, and eventually the east side, were developed with houses in the seventeenth and eighteenth centuries. Most of the buildings seen on the north side date from the eighteenth or early nineteenth centuries, but the Rose and Crown had been rebuilt with a Tudor gable. The shaft visible in the centre is the stand pipe tower of the Kew Bridge water pumping station in Brentford (now the Kew Bridge Steam Museum). (Photograph by E.J. Haywood)

FLORA HOUSE, 81 KEW GREEN, now a private residence. Many of the houses round the Green were restaurants or tea gardens before the First World War. This was one of the best known. Will Evans, the proprietor, is believed to be the man on the left of the gate.

NOS 17/19 KEW GREEN, originally (and now again) one house, had been divided into two long before this photograph was taken in 1951. The run-down state of this early-eighteenth century property was somewhat typical of Kew just after the war.

DEMOLITION OF THE SECOND KEW BRIDGE, 1899–1900. The first bridge at Kew, a wooden structure, was opened in 1759. It was replaced by a stone bridge in 1789.

THE THIRD (AND PRESENT) KEW BRIDGE, while construction was still in progress in May 1903.

KEW GREEN, THE NORTH-EAST END near the bridge, in the late nineteenth century. The house on the far left and the blacksmith's forge were both demolished when the new bridge was built.

KEW GREEN, FROM THE END OF KEW ROAD, C. 1939, a photograph taken soon after the widening of the road and the rebuilding of the shops on the left (now the Pissarro Wine Bar).

GLOUCESTER HOUSE, KEW ROAD in 1909. Built about 1750, the house was occupied by George III's brother, the Duke of Gloucester. It became Neumagen's Jewish School in 1840, then a girls' school, run by the Neumagens. The site is now flats – Gloucester Court.

GLOUCESTER COTTAGES, KEW ROAD in 1899. Built in the eighteenth century for workers in Kew Palace Gardens, they were demolished when Kew Road was widened.

'THE BARN CHURCH' (St Philip's and All Saints'), North Sheen, 1929. North Sheen was transferred from Mortlake to Richmond in 1892. The area east of Kew station was developed in the 1920s. A church was provided by the re-erection of a sixteenth-century barn from a Surrey farm.

Richmond, East and North of the Green

THE BLACK HORSE, at the corner of Sheen Road and Queen's Road, is one of Richmond's oldest public houses still trading under the same name and in the same place. It was opened early in the eighteenth century at Marshgate, where a gate stood across the road to East Sheen, on the Mortlake boundary. The land here was originally very marshy. The photograph was taken in August 1904 by a Miss Peirce, before the pub was rebuilt.

FARM BUILDINGS ON GROVE ROAD. The farm was run by the Stanford family, descendants of George III's chief shepherd at Richmond.

THE MARSHGATE ARMS stood until 1907 where Marshgate, now Sheen, Road (left) and Worple Way (right) divided.

IRELANDS' SHOP at 19 Sheen Road when first opened in 1886.

THE LOWER END OF THE SHEEN ROAD, c. 1890. The building on the left, originally the single-storey Mechanics' Institute built in 1843, acquired a dome in 1908, and then became a cinema. Behind it is the fire station.

'BUG ISLAND' in the 1880s. The group of cottages and shops between George Street and Lower George Street had degenerated into a slum, nicknamed 'Bug Island', by the late nineteenth century. Most were rebuilt in 1890.

OBELISK AND WATER PUMP IN GEORGE STREET, 1904. On the left is the new bank building replacing the shops seen on the previous page. The seventeenth-century gable of Long's was part of the old Castle Inn.

THE CORNER OF DUKE STREET AND THE QUADRANT, c. 1860.

DUKE STREET got its name from Mr William Duke who owned a large house on the north side in the early seventeenth century. The upper picture shows, on the left, the Baptist church built in 1880–81. It was replaced by a modern church building in 1961–2. Below is the south side of the street in December 1903, showing the Cobwebs, a public house dating from the early nineteenth century. It still exists, rebuilt, and renamed (in 1990) the 'Racing Page'.

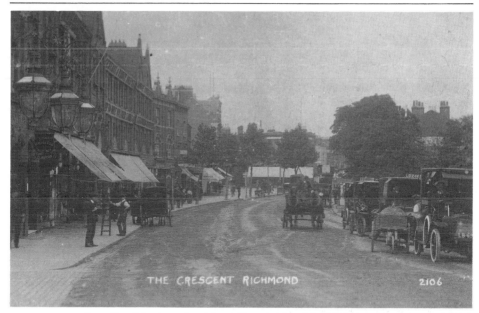

THE CRESCENT, Kew Road, just north of the railway bridge. The LSWR station was on the left (see p. 106). The cabs are waiting outside the District Railway station on the right.

THE CORNER OF KEW ROAD AND THE LOWER MORTLAKE ROAD before the building of the roundabout and the Chertsey Road in the 1930s.

THE SUN INN, PARKSHOT, 1909. Parkshot was then continuous with the Kew Foot Road. The Sun Inn, first recorded in 1732, rebuilt in 1842, has changed little in outward appearance.

NOS 7, 8 AND 9 PARKSHOT, January 1899. This row of eighteenth-century houses was pulled down in 1900 and is now the site of the Magistrates' Court. George Eliot lived in No. 8 from 1856 to 1858, while writing *Scenes from Clerical Life* and part of *Adam Bede*.

The Centre of Richmond

LITTLE GREEN, RICHMOND, with its Crimean War cannon, photographed at a date between 1881 when the Public Library (seen on the right) was built and 1899 when the new Richmond Theatre was built. The northern end of the Green was gradually reduced by encroachment of houses and of the royal gardens until only a small square was left as 'Little Green'. The houses seen on the left of the picture are all that now remains of the development by John Price in 1712–25.

THE SOUTH SIDE OF RICHMOND GREEN BY NIGHT. Most of the houses here date from the eighteenth century, and are now used as offices. The street lamp on the left is by the end of Brewer's Lane – Richmond's shopping centre in the time of the first Queen Elizabeth. (Photograph by G.W. Cockram)

NOS 11–20 THE GREEN. Nos 11 and 12 on the left, built about 1715, are notable for their finely-carved doorcases and cornices. The house with a pediment, No. 17, was Richmond's principal coffee house in the eighteenth century.

DOORWAYS, NO. 22 THE GREEN. This pair of houses, built in 1724 on the site of the White Horse Tavern, has recently been restored, after being used for many years as an annexe to the post office.

THE PRINCE'S HEAD at the corner of the Green and Paved Court. The tavern, originally called the Duke of Ormond's Head, was first recorded in 1705. Later it became the Duke's Head, and then the Prince's Head. In 1902, when the photograph was taken, the proprietor was Bill East, royal barge-master and champion sculler.

OLD PALACE TERRACE, OAK HOUSE AND OLD PALACE PLACE, in the snow. Old Palace Terrace was built by William Wollins in 1692 for the London lawyer Vertue Radford. Radord's own house, Old Palace Place, was refronted about the same time. Oak House, built in the 1760s, was originally an extension to Old Palace Place.

KING STREET held many early inns and taverns. By the time of this photograph, in May 1900, the Feathers, on the left, one of the most famous, had become an office. The Old Ship, on the right, which is still in business, had already been flourishing for over two centuries.

880   RICHMOND. — King Street.' — LL.

LOOKING DOWN KING STREET towards the Green about 1910. The Queen's Head, absorbed into Gosling's store in 1960, and the buildings beyond it have all now been replaced by the new Dickins and Jones store.

873   RICHMOND. — *George Street*. — LL.

GEORGE STREET, LOOKING NORTH-EAST, about 1905. King Street and George Street were officially so named in 1769 in honour of Richmond's royal resident and patron. George Street had become the main shopping street of Richmond by the late seventeenth century. Gosling's department store, on the left, started as a drapery in 1795 and gradually expanded, taking over adjacent shops and the Queen's Head Hotel. The tallest building on the right is Wright Brothers' store. At the end of the road the tall chimney of the electrical power station can be seen. Its stub is still visible by the entrance to the multi-storey car park at Richmond station.

FIRE AT 49, 50 AND 50A GEORGE STREET, 12 September 1900. No. 49, Lilley and Skinners' shoe shop, had to be rebuilt. Nos 50 and 50A survived. They are today almost the only eighteenth-century buildings left in George Street.

GEORGE STREET, LOOKING SOUTH-WEST, early twentieth century. Note the dome on Wright Brothers (later Owen Owen), and the tall, rebuilt No. 49 on the right.

PARADISE ROAD AND THE END OF CHURCH TERRACE in 1907. Facing the churchyard, in 1907, were these sheds and workrooms, at the end of the dignified eighteenth-century houses of Church Terrace.

THE RED LION TAVERN. The Red Lyon, the main inn of Tudor times, at the corner of Red Lion Street and George Street, closed down in the 1720s. About 1755 the name was revived for this tavern, further up Red Lion Street. It was demolished in 1909.

NO. 1 LONG'S BUILDINGS (demolished 1909) was reached from Ormond Passage, an alleyway from the Red Lion to Ormond Road. Built in the mid-eighteenth century, this house (whose bay gives it a curiously 1930s appearance) contained one of Richmond's best plaster ceilings.

THE CORNER OF ORMOND ROAD, PATTEN ALLEY (left) AND ORMOND PASSAGE (right) in October 1900. The Independent (Calvinist) Bethlehem chapel, built in 1797, can be seen on the far right, facing on to Ormond Passage.

THE SOUTH SIDE OF ORMOND ROAD, 1901, with its early-eighteenth-century houses, has changed little. However, those at the end now face the Odeon Cinema.

THE MAIDS OF HONOUR SHOP in Hill Street was opened about 1700. The secret recipe for the little cheese-flavoured tartlets called 'Maids of Honour' was handed on from one proprietor to the next. The shop-front was removed about 1957, when the name (and the recipe) were taken over by the Newens Bakery in Kew.

NOS 9/11 HILL STREET were built for Ellis's wine business, with a meeting hall on the upper floor. Richmond's first bank – the London and County – opened there In 1852. Rebuilt after bombing in 1940, the premises now house the National Westminster Bank.

RICHMOND TOWN HALL was built on the site of the Castle Hotel, presented to the new borough by Sir John Whittaker Ellis. It was opened in June 1893.

THE FIRST RICHMOND COUNCIL. Richmond was chartered as a Borough on 16 July 1890, and the first Council was elected in November. Sir John Whittaker Ellis, MP and a former Lord Mayor of London, became the first mayor. Seated are (from left to right) Aldermen Roberts, Burt, Cook, Mayor Ellis, Aldermen Robinson, Szlumper, Piggott and Gascoyne. Alderman Skewes-Cox is standing at far right.

HERON HOUSE, much altered and renovated, survives in the new Riverside development as a reminder of a redevelopment project of the 1690s. Emma Hamilton lived in this house in 1809–10. Heron Court was originally 'Herring Court', but Joseph Harvey in the 1840s adorned his house with figures of herons, and called it Heron House. In the 1850s the street name was changed. The photographs were taken in March 1908 by N.S. Hopkins.

Hill Street and Town Hall   Richmond

HILL STREET. Above, Ellis's building with the meeting hall dominated the western side of the street. The old Feathers Inn building closes the vista. The shops on the right were demolished when the upper end of the street was widened about 1930. Below, the corner of Bridge Street and 'Royal Terrace', built in 1838.

SECTION FOUR

Palace and Riverside

THE GATEWAY OF RICHMOND PALACE. Above the gate are the arms of Henry VII who rebuilt the palace in 1498–1501. The only parts remaining of the Tudor palace (largely demolished in the 1650s) are the gateway and part of the house adjoining it, and the Wardrobe building, which is on the left through the gate. The oriel window above the gateway was an eighteenth-century addition, removed when the building was restored in 1939.

TRUMPETERS' HOUSE was built in 1703–4 on the site of the Middle Gate of the Tudor palace. The splendid portico was added about 1745. The croquet players on the lawn are playing where the state apartments once stood.

ONE OF THE TWO TRUMPETER FIGURES which once adorned the Middle Gate of the palace, and then Trumpeters' House. Both had already lost their right arms and trumpets when photographed by N.S. Hopkins in September 1905. They still stand by the door of Trumpeters' Lodge.

OLD PALACE YARD in 1900, looking northward from Trumpeters' House. On the left are stables and workshops replaced with houses in 1950.

OLD PALACE LANE with its late-eighteenth-century cottages has changed little.

THE RICHMOND LOCK AND WEIR AND THE NEW FOOTBRIDGE, just prior to their opening by the Duke of York (the future King George V) on 19 May 1894. The photograph, from the programme for the opening ceremony, is taken from the Twickenham bank; and the Richmond railway bridge can be seen in the background.

ASGILL HOUSE, built in 1762 for Sir Charles Asgill, Lord Mayor of London, by Sir Robert Taylor, lost its original elegance when the wings were built up an extra storey and other extensions added for Benjamin Cohen in the mid-nineteenth century. It was restored to the original plan in 1970 by the present owner. Below, the octagonal drawing-room in its Victorian decoration.

WHITECROSS ROW, built in the 1790s, was a row of eighteen cottages running back from the river by the White Cross Hotel. Many of its inhabitants were watermen and boat builders. At No. 6 was the Jolly Anglers Tea Rooms. (Photograph dated November 1902)

WATER LANE today still retains its old paving, with granite setts for the wheels of the drays from Collins' brewery and cobbles for the horses' hooves. The brewery buildings are on the right. Half-way up on the left is the Waterman's Arms. The old timber building at the top of the lane was part of the former Feathers Inn.

RICHMOND RIVERSIDE, 1952. The former offices of Collins' brewery, which can be seen in the photographs of 1840 and 1856 on pp. 6 and 7, had become the headquarters of Richmond's municipal water supply operation in 1876, and were still so used in 1952. Beyond were boathouses, then still flourishing, but now replaced by a restaurant in the new development. Tower House, in the background, survives to give its special signature to the Richmond Riverside view.

RICHMOND BRIDGE FROM CHOLMONDELEY WALK, c. 1900. The barges moored along the river bank, the river steamer at its pier, the shoals of rowing boats on the river waiting to be hired, give an impression of great river activity. Who was the gentleman in the top hat and morning suit? A passenger from the steamer, a curious visitor, or the proprietor of some business expecting a delivery by barge?

RICHMOND BRIDGE, 1856. This view by George Hilditch shows the old toll-gates and toll-houses. Tower House, built to the design of Henry Laxton, is just nearing completion (note the builders' paint marks on the new window glass).

TOWER HOUSE. An artist was brought specially from Italy to paint the designs on the walls of some of the rooms of Tower House.

THE TOLL-HOUSES ON RICHMOND BRIDGE were demolished after 1859 when the bridge became free. The upper photograph is by George Hilditch, about 1856. The lower photograph appears to pre-date the building of Tower House in 1856.

SECTION FIVE

Richmond Hill

THE JUNCTION OF HILL RISE AND THE PETERSHAM ROAD. All the buildings on the long thin triangle of land north of Compass Hill have now been demolished, some when Petersham Road (on the right) was widened in the 1930s, those on the upper side in 1966–7. On the left part of Holbrook House can be seen, and then the adjacent houses before their conversion into shops. In the centre of the picture is a magnificent piece of street furniture – the wrought-iron lamppost – and beyond it a public water fountain.

LOOKING DOWN HILL RISE to the Bridge Street corner. Among the shops on the left are five tea rooms. There are now five restaurants.

COTTAGES IN THE PETERSHAM ROAD, c. 1902.

THE COMPASSES HOTEL from which Compass Hill derived its name. This tavern was originally the Rising Sun; the name was transferred in the 1780s from the old Three Compasses at the top of the Hill.

THE BRITISH LEGION POPPY FACTORY in the Petersham Road before rebuilding in 1970. The Armistice Day poppies have been made in Richmond since their inception.

VINE ROW COTTAGES IN LANCASTER ROAD. The whitewashed eighteenth-century cottages still remain, but the workshops beyond them have recently been replaced by new houses. There were originally similar cottages on the opposite side of the road, but these were pulled down to be replaced by an additional wing of Michel's Almshouses in 1858. In the background is St Elizabeth's church.

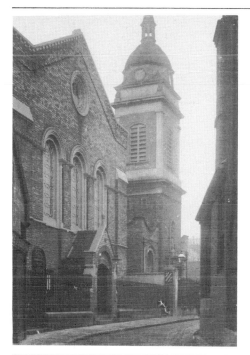

THE CONGREGATIONAL CHURCH AND ST ELIZA-BETH'S ROMAN CATHOLIC CHURCH IN THE VINE-YARD. St Elizabeth's was built at the expense of Miss Elizabeth Doughty in 1824. It was much altered and enlarged, with a new tower, in 1903. The Congregational church was built in 1831 in a 'romanesque' style, and was rebuilt after a fire in 1851.

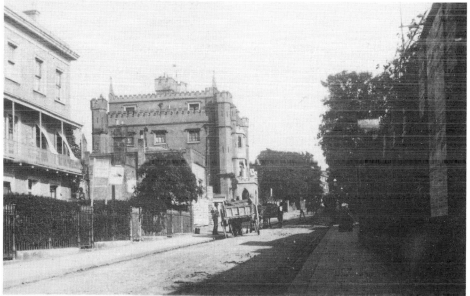

OLD VICARAGE SCHOOL, RICHMOND HILL. This house was in origin a late seventeenth-century mansion. It was the home of the Houblon family until the 1780s. Mrs Ellerker bought the house in 1808 and had it 'gothicized'. It has been a school since the 1880s; the Old Vicarage School moved here in 1931.

Left:

ST MATTHIAS'S CHURCH, one of the new churches built for the expanding population of Richmond, was designed by Sir Gilbert Scott, and was consecrated on 7 August 1858. This photograph of 1875 shows, on the left, a villa in Friars Stile Road (destroyed by bombing in the Second World War).

Below:

THE WESLEYAN CHAPEL IN FRIARS STILE ROAD was built in 1850 as an appendage to the Wesleyan Training College (now Richmond College). It was destroyed by bombing in 1940. (Photograph by R.R. Phillips, 1903)

THE TERRACE, RICHMOND HILL. The stables next to the Roebuck Inn were replaced about 1865 by the large mansion called 'Terrace House' built for Mr Charles Bell. The Roebuck was an established tavern by 1720.

EASTER PARADE ON THE TERRACE. On the right is Doughty House with its conservatory.

WICK HOUSE before the Second World War. Who could discern, beneath all this Victorian decoration, the simple villa built in 1771–2 for Sir Joshua Reynolds by Sir William Chambers? The tower wing was added, and the front altered, in the middle of the nineteenth century. When this photograph was taken, the house was an annexe for the Richmond Hill Hotel. In 1948 it was bought by the Royal Star and Garter Home for use as a nurses' home, and was restored (though without complete removal of the tower) to something approaching its original appearance.

REGENCY HOUSES ON RICHMOND HILL. Nos 1/3 Mansfield Place (above) are now part of the Richmond Hill Hotel. Below, the houses now forming the Richmond Gate Hotel – even the two cottages on the left, built in the 1720s, have been 'Regency-fied'! (Photos by R.R. Phillips, 1915)

THE FOUNTAIN ON RICHMOND HILL was erected in 1891 as a memorial to the Duchess of Teck, mother of Queen Mary, who lived at White Lodge in Richmond Park.

THE LASS OF RICHMOND HILL in March 1900, shortly before rebuilding. The tavern, established in the 1840s, took the name of the popular song. Though it was long believed that the 'Lass' belonged to Richmond in Yorkshire, recent research has shown there were no grounds for this. There was probably no particular Lass; it was just a good song.

SECTION SIX

Petersham

RICHMOND HILL AND PETERSHAM MEADOWS AND COMMON, c. 1900. On the left of the picture is Richmond: Devonshire Lodge near the river was demolished in 1968; above is Doughty House on the Terrace and to its right the great round bay of The Wick (built in 1775). In the centre the Mansion Hotel shows through the trees. Everything to the right of this is in Petersham. The view is dominated by the Star and Garter Hotel.

THE STAR AND GARTER HOTEL AND PETERSHAM ALMSHOUSES. In the upper picture (c. 1860) the hotel is seen before the addition of the Barry building in 1865. It had been enlarged by Joseph Ellis in the 1820s. The almshouses had been moved from a higher position to their site by the Petersham Road in 1809. The lower photograph shows hotel and almshouses rebuilt; the former in 1865 and 1874, the latter in 1866. The almshouses were finally pulled down in 1953.

THE PETERSHAM ROAD AND HILL in the 1920s. The greatest change today is the traffic! In the lower picture the Russell School can be seen (see p. 137). It was destroyed by a bomb in 1943.

THE RUSSELL BRITISH SCHOOL AND THE BUTE HOUSE GATES, c. 1875. The vehicles parked near the entrance to Bute House are probably the carriages of picnic parties visiting Petersham Park, the gate to which was just behind the school. Bute House was demolished at the end of the nineteenth century.

FOUNTAIN COTTAGE, the tuckshop for the school, was on the opposite side of the Petersham Road. Crossing the road would have been no problem then.

OLD WOODEN BUILDINGS, PETERSHAM VALE. These stood just to the east of the Dysart Arms until demolished in 1896. They may have been part of the farm of which the pub was originally the farmhouse. The shed with the pantile roof is very much part of the Petersham building vernacular. Several existing cottages had similar roofs until quite recently.

THE DYSART ARMS in 1902. From about 1750 till 1804 the inn was known as the Plough and Harrow. The name was changed at the behest of the Countess of Dysart, living at Ham House. The picture can be compared with the one of fifty years earlier on p. 10; there is little change, even in the window boxes! The lower picture shows the yard at the rear.

THE DYSART ARMS BY NIGHT, 1948. The old inn was rebuilt in 1902 in a mock-Tudor style. As rebuilt it still stands, but has recently changed its name again, to The Dysarts. (Photograph by H.W. Hyde)

ST PETER'S CHURCH is mentioned in the Domesday Book. The oldest part of the present building, in the north wall of the chancel, dates from about AD 1200. The church is wider than it is long, large transepts having been added in the seventeenth and nineteenth centuries. The interior still retains its nineteenth-century box pews and gallery. The grandparents of Her Majesty the Queen were married in the church in 1881.

ALL SAINTS' CHURCH INTERIOR, 1908. In 1894 Mrs Lionel Warde of Petersham House bought the Bute House estate. She built the huge All Saints' church in 'Romanesque' style as a memorial to her parents, and to be the centre of a large population which never developed. The church was never consecrated; and was used as a radar school in the Second World War.

PETERSHAM HOUSE was built in the late seventeenth century. The upper floor and the fine porch were added in the nineteenth century. Owners of the house in the eighteenth century included Robert Manners and Lucy, Duchess of Montrose. (Photograph by N.S. Hopkins, 1905)

RUTLAND LODGE, built at the beginning of the eighteenth century, derives its name from Lucy, Duchess of Rutland. Gutted by fire in 1967, it was converted into flats. (Photograph by R.R. Phillips, 1903)

THE GLEN, RIVER LANE was the home from 1796 until his death in 1798 of Captain George Vancouver. Here he wrote up his account of his voyages of discovery.

VANCOUVER ANNIVERSARY, 1948. The grave of Vancouver in Petersham churchyard is the scene of an annual ceremony on the anniversary of his burial. The 150th anniversary was in 1948, and the ceremony was attended by both the Lord Mayor of London and the Canadian High Commissioner (see also p. 159).

FARM LODGE, Petersham Road, is a surviving relic of the great estate of Petersham Lodge which stood where Petersham Park is today. A room was used as the Petersham branch library 1900–08. (Photograph January 1900)

THE FOX AND DUCK INN, 1910. The old inn seen here was rebuilt about 1940. Adjacent to it is the timber watch house and lock-up.

PETERSHAM STORES, 1908. Petersham no longer has a village shop; but in the nineteenth century distinguished customers included the Dukes of Clarence and Cambridge, Charles Dickens and William Thackeray. Myrtle Cottage, on the left, still stands – little changed except for the iron railings which were contributed to the war effort.

DOUGLAS HOUSE, built in the 1680s, was famous as the home of Kitty Hyde, Duchess of Queensberry. The house was bought by the German Government in 1969, and a German school has been built in the grounds.

HAM HOUSE, built in 1610 for Sir Thomas Vavasour. It was the home of the Tollemache family, Earls of Dysart, and of the Duke of Lauderdale. The National Trust have restored the gardens to their seventeenth-century layout.

Ham

HAM MANOR HOUSE, a Queen Anne house, has not been greatly altered, and maintains its seclusion behind high brick walls. Among its best-known residents were Christine, daughter of Lucien Bonaparte, and Sir George Gilbert Scott, the famous Victorian architect.

SHOPS IN THE PETERSHAM ROAD, 1910. These shops, now demolished, stood near the Ham boundary stone. Slades' sweet shop is second from the right and further down is Hills' bakery.

THE POND ON HAM COMMON, c. 1900. On the left in the background is Ensleigh Lodge and next to it the old malthouse with its louvred ventilator. To the right of the tree is St Andrew's School, and to its right Selby House, built in 1688.

THE TOLLGATE HOUSE, UPPER HAM ROAD, 1891. The gatehouse was erected in 1771 and restored in 1892 and again in 1968. At the door stands Sarah ('Grannie') Morfew, daughter of a Farnham charcoal burner, who lived in the house for forty years until her death, aged 104, in 1892. Notice the pump on the left of the picture, one of several public hand pumps in the village.

ST ANDREW'S CHURCH, HAM. Ham had no church until 1832, when St Andrew's was built on ground granted by the Countess of Dysart. The architect was Edward Lapidge. The south aisle was added in 1857, and a new chancel in 1900. (Photograph by R.R. Phillips, 1915)

LATCHMERE HOUSE, 1900. An early Victorian house which has had a variety of institutional uses: a convalescent home for the shell-shocked in the First World War; an interrogation centre in the Second World War; and, ever since, a remand centre.

LAMMAS LANDS IN HAM MEADOWS. George Greenwood and his son in their flower fields. The meadows were reduced by the digging of gravel pits; then the new Ham estates in the 1950s and '60s covered all but an outer fringe.

THE OLD LOCK HOUSE. Teddington locks were first built in 1811, with the lock-keeper's house on the Ham bank of the river. The locks were enlarged in 1854 and 1904.

AN AERIAL VIEW OF HAM, 1944. Ham Street runs down the right side of the picture, with Ham Common and its pond visible in the bottom right corner. The most striking feature is the gravel pits, exploited by the Dysarts from 1900 to 1952. Invasion barges (and, it is said, sections of the Mulberry Harbour) were stored in the flooded pits during the Second World War. (© British Crown copyright/MOD.)

Richmond Park

WHITE LODGE was ordered by George I and finished for George II. Designed by Roger Morris, it was subsequently altered by the addition of the wings and crescent corridors for Princess Amelia when she was Ranger of the Park from 1751 to 1761. It was further altered in 1802 to make a residence for George III's prime minister, Henry Addington, Viscount Sidmouth, who was Deputy Ranger from 1813 until his death in 1844. Occupied briefly by the Duke and Duchess of York (King George VI and Queen Elizabeth) after their marriage, it is now the home of the Royal Ballet School.

RICHMOND GATE AND LODGES, built to the designs of Sir John Soane in 1798–9, are seen in this photograph before their alteration to take increased road traffic in 1896.

THE BANDSTAND IN RICHMOND PARK was erected near the Richmond Gate in 1931. It was similar in design to one also built at that time in Kensington Gardens. In 1975 the bandstand, which had been unused for many years, was moved to Regent's Park.

SHEEN LODGE OR COTTAGE was originally the dog kennels for the royal buckhounds. In 1787 the Rt. Hon. William Adam obtained a lease, and the huntsman's cottage was converted into a large residence. From 1852 to 1892 it was the home of Sir Richard Owen, first director of the Natural History Museum.

PEMBROKE LODGE in October 1902, originally the Molecatcher's cottage. In 1780 Elizabeth, Countess of Pembroke, rented lodgings there. She was later granted the whole house and had substantial alterations made to it by Sir John Soane. In 1847 the house was granted to Lord John Russell.

PETERSHAM PARK, originally separated from Richmond Park as the grounds of Petersham Lodge, was reunited with the Park in 1835. The area was set aside for school outings and picnics.

Some Vanished Stately Homes

SPRING GROVE at the bottom end of Queen's Road was the residence of Sir Charles Rugge Price Bt, when this photograph was taken in March 1899. The mansion was built for the Marquess of Lothian in the early eighteenth century, but many additions were made later. It was occupied by seven generations of the Price family from 1797 until demolished in 1927.

UPPER DUNSTABLE HOUSE on the north side of the Sheen Road was built in the mid-eighteenth century for Dr John Baker, a well-known physician. The Baker family lived in it until the 1860s. It was demolished in 1909. (Photograph 1906)

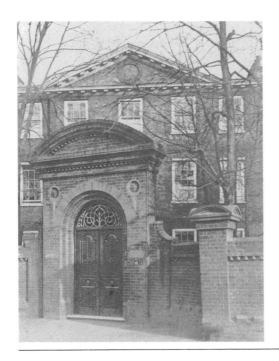

LICHFIELD HOUSE in the Sheen Road was replaced by the Lichfield Court flats in 1935. The house, built in the early eighteenth century, took its name from James Cornwallis, Bishop of Lichfield, who lived in it until his death in 1824. A later occupant (1865 to 1915) was the novelist Mary Elizabeth Braddon.

CARRINGTON HOUSE (above) and EGERTON HOUSE (below) in photographs by N.S. Hopkins, December 1907. Egerton House, in the corner between Sheen Road and Paradise Road, was demolished in the 1930s. Carrington Lodge, a late-seventeenth-century mansion, was the home in the early nineteenth century of Colonel Robert Carrington Smith (later Lord Carrington). It was later divided into three, the wings becoming Streatham Lodge and Beverley Lodge. Used during the Second World War as a British Restaurant, it was demolished shortly after the war.

QUEENSBERRY HOUSE in October 1907. The Marquess Cholmondeley's mansion by the riverside, built in the 1730s, was owned by the Duke of Queensberry ('Old Q') from 1780 to 1810. It was pulled down in 1831 and a new Queensberry House was built, further back from the river, for Sir William Dundas Bt. This house was replaced by the existing Queensberry House flats in 1934.

HOTHAM HOUSE was built in the 1690s. The name derives from Admiral Hotham, resident from about 1810 to 1820. In 1960 the house, then used by the Borough Engineer's Department, started to collapse and had to be demolished.

BRIDGE HOUSE was built c. 1690 for the Revd Abiel Borfett, minister of Richmond. Before its demolition in the 1950s it had become a café, whose terraces facing the river were a delightful place for tea in the summer.

NORTHUMBERLAND HOUSE, Petersham Road, built in 1766 for the dramatist George Colman, was occupied by the Dowager Duchess of Northumberland in the 1870s. It was demolished in 1969.

GOTHIC HOUSE, Petersham Road, was built about 1810 and one of its first occupants was Madame de Stael. The house was pulled down when the Petersham Road was widened in 1938.

CARDIGAN HOUSE on Richmond Hill was built in 1791–3 by Robert Mylne for Mr Robert Sayer. While rented to the Duke of Clarence it was damaged by fire in 1797. The house took its name from the 5th and 6th Earls of Cardigan who lived there from about 1805 to 1837. In 1950 the council acquired part of the grounds to add to the Terrace Gardens, and the house was then used as a British Legion clubhouse until its demolition in 1970.

BUCCLEUCH HOUSE, built in 1761–2 by the 4th Earl of Cardigan (later Duke of Montagu), was inherited by his daughter the Duchess of Buccleuch in 1790. In 1887 Sir John Whittaker Ellis purchased the house from the Buccleuch family, and the Richmond Vestry acquired most of its grounds to open them to the public as Terrace Gardens. The house was bought by the council in 1937 and demolished.

BUTE HOUSE, Petersham, the home from 1795 to 1832 of the 1st Marquess of Bute and his wife. The house was purchased and demolished in 1894 by Mrs Lionel Warde of Petersham House (see p. 73).

The Famous Hotels

THE GREYHOUND HOTEL in George Street was, in the eighteenth and nineteenth centuries, one of the two principal inns in the centre of Richmond. It survived as a hotel into the age of the motor car and the telephone. The building was renovated as offices, Greyhound House, in 1983–4.

THE CASTLE HOTEL, Hill Street, with grounds stretching to the riverside, photographed shortly before demolition in 1888. Its site was presented to the town by Sir John Whittaker Ellis for the new municipal offices. Above, the entrance in Hill Street; below,.the back, facing the river.

THE RICHMOND HILL HOTEL'S ORIGINAL BUILDING was Mansfield House, the central block of which was built in the 1720s. The wings were added by the Countess of Mansfield who occupied the house from 1813 to 1843. It was converted to become the Queen's Hotel in 1875, and changed its name to Richmond Hill Hotel in 1913.

THE OLD BUILDING OF THE STAR AND GARTER HOTEL, c. 1865. The famous Star and Garter started as a small pub built on the edge of Petersham Common, outside the Park gate, in 1738. It was enlarged in the 1770s and the building seen here was built by Richard Brewer in 1803.

STAR AND GARTER: THE BARRY BUILDING. When a limited company took over from the Ellis family in 1864, it replaced the older parts by a new building in 'French-château' style, designed by E.M. Barry. Barry also designed a new banqueting hall, added at the north end of the 1803 building.

STAR AND GARTER: THE 'PAVILION'. The 1803 building was destroyed by a fire in 1870, which left the 1860s additions largely undamaged. It was replaced in 1874 by 'a pavilion in the Italian Romanesque style' designed by C.J. Phipps.

STAR AND GARTER. Above, the new pavilion stood between the 1865 banqueting hall (left) and the 'château' block (right). Below, the dining room, seating 250, in the pavilion.

THE MANSION HOTEL, now the Petersham, still stands. Built on the slopes of the Hill below the Star and Garter in 1865, it was first called the Richmond Hill Hotel. It changed its name to the Mansion in 1877, the (New) Star and Garter in 1924, and finally the Petersham in 1978. The architect was John Giles, who also built the Langham Hotel in Portland Place. It has a notable tall stone staircase, with ceiling murals.

Transport

A THAMES BARGE NEAR RICHMOND BRIDGE.

A RIVER STEAMER in the 1890s. From about 1815 steamboats began to appear on the river at Richmond, carrying passengers both up- and down-stream. The paddle-wheeler in this picture was a typical late-nineteenth-century vessel. Also seen is a small steam launch and many rowing boats for hire by day trippers.

A COACH IN THE SHEEN ROAD.

TRAFFIC CONGESTION AT THE BOTTOM OF HILL STREET.

THE LONDON AND SOUTH WESTERN RAILWAY STATION, built in 1853 between the Kew Road and Parkshot, photographed on 20 July 1936, not long before its demolition.

THE TERMINAL STATION AT RICHMOND used by the District and North London services was built in 1869. The LSWR's through tracks are in the foreground.

A LONDON AND SOUTH WESTERN RAILWAY TRAIN approaching Richmond.

A DISTRICT RAILWAY LOCOMOTIVE, c. 1880. The Church Road bridge is in the background. The extra external pipework was a steam-condensation system, designed to reduce the emission of steam in the underground sections of the line.

CYCLING. This view of Richmond Bridge shows three different cycles in use: a penny-farthing bicycle, an early 'modern' bicycle, and a tricycle.

THE RICHMOND CYCLE STORES in Duke Street must have caused some road congestion if this was a typical scene.

A HORSE BUS outside the Orange Tree pub in Kew Road. This bus plied between Richmond and Kingston on the route now followed by the No. 65 bus.

A HORSE TRAM outside the depot in the Kew Road. To go to Kew from Richmond one did not take a bus, but a tram. One terminus was at the end of Kew Bridge, the other here in Kew Road.

MOTOR BUSES ON RICHMOND BRIDGE. Whether the four buses, nose to tail, at the stop outside the King's Arms and waiting by the Talbot Hotel on Hill Street to turn on to the bridge, represented a better service or just a characteristic bunching, they were evidently all well crowded. The photograph is not dated, but might be about 1914.

Theatres and Picture Palaces

THE THEATRE ROYAL on Richmond Green, built in 1765, was Richmond's third theatre. The two earlier ones had both been on the Hill. Many famous actors performed here, including Garrick (who spoke the prologue for the opening), Dorothy Jordan, William Charles Macready, Sarah Siddons, Edmund Kean and Helen Faucit. Kean, who managed the theatre from 1831 to 1833, died in the manager's house adjoining the theatre, on the right in the picture. The theatre was demolished in 1884–5.

THE ASSEMBLY ROOMS OF THE CASTLE HOTEL were used as a theatre from 1890 to 1899. In 1910 they became Richmond's first cinema – the Castle Electric Theatre.

RICHMOND THEATRE on Little Green was opened in 1899. It was designed by Frank Matcham, the famous theatre architect. This photograph dates from the early 1900s.

THE TALBOT PICTURE THEATRE, the first purpose-built cinema in Richmond, was opened in March 1911, adjoining the Talbot Hotel. It was closed in April 1930, replaced by the Richmond Kinema next door.

THE GAUMONT CINEMA in Hill Street, was originally the New Royalty Kinema. It was opened on Christmas Eve, 1914, with a new auditorium built behind Hill Street. In 1944 the cinema was bought by Odeon Theatres and renamed the Gaumont. It was closed in 1980; the house has been renovated as offices.

THE INTERIOR OF THE RICHMOND KINEMA (now the Odeon) as it was when opened in April 1930. Renamed the Premier in 1940, it was sold to Odeon Theatres in 1944 and again renamed as the Odeon. It still stands, but its division into three smaller auditoriums means that much of the original decor has been destroyed.

THE RITZ (LATER ABC) CINEMA in Sheen Road was opened in May 1938. It was closed in December 1971 and replaced by the office block called Spencer House.

SECTION THIRTEEN

People at Play

BOATING ON THE RIVER. This photograph shows not only the Thames barges moored two deep against the river bank, but the popularity of 'boating' on the river at the turn of the century.

BOATS FOR HIRE along the riverside between Richmond Bridge and the White Cross Hotel.

THE RIVER FROM PETERSHAM MEADOWS. This photograph (by J.B. Hilditch, George's son) shows two other forms of river craft: the small steam launch and the punt. Punts were rare at Richmond.

THE GREAT THAMES SWIM, from Richmond Lock to Blackfriars Bridge, was inaugurated in 1907. In July 1908, recorded in these pictures from the *Graphic*, there were thirty-seven starters including six women. Eighteen completed the whole course – fourteen-and-a-half miles. The winner was a Leicester man, J.A. Jarvis, in a time of 3 hours, 36 minutes, 24 seconds.

THEY'RE OFF!

CRICKET ON HAM COMMON, Whit Monday 1930. Cricket is recorded as having been played on Richmond Green as long ago as 1665. The Ham and Petersham Cricket Club is said to have been formed about 1815, though the earliest recorded match on Ham Common was in 1841.

CRICKET MATCH ON KEW GREEN between the Tradesmen of Kew and the Tradesmen of Richmond. This charity match was played on behalf of the Richmond Royal Hospital.

INTERNATIONAL CONTESTS AT THE RICHMOND ATHLETICS GROUND. The Athletics Ground, established in a corner of the Old Deer Park in 1886, soon became a site for international sports. Rugby Union Internationals were played here before the Twickenham ground was built. The England–France match in 1908 is pictured above.

THE LADIES' HOCKEY MATCH between England and Scotland in 1913.

THE ROYAL RICHMOND HORSE SHOW was inaugurated in 1892 and was held annually, except in wartime, until 1967. The photograph above shows the committee in 1894. The Horse Show, under royal patronage, was one of the events of the London season. Below, King George V and Queen Mary arriving at the show in 1913.

THE CARRIAGE DRIVING EVENT at the Royal Richmond Horse Show, 1965.

A GOLF MATCH between Harry Lauder and Harry Taylor in 1913. The Mid-Surrey Golf Club was founded on 24 October 1892, with a course in the Old Deer Park. Harry Taylor (on the left), an open golf champion, was the club's most famous professional. Harry Lauder was the renowned Scots comedian.

People at Work

UNLOADING A BARGE. The muddy foreshore suggests that this undated photograph pre-dates the building of Richmond weir. A strong horse must have been needed to pull this quite small cart, when laden with bricks, up the ramp from the foreshore to the roadway by the riverside.

BOATBUILDING was an important Richmond trade, often carried on by the proprietors of the hire fleets from the boathouses along the riverbank.

MESSUM'S BOATYARD, next to the Three Pigeons public house on the Petersham Road.

THE CHIMNEY SWEEP. Colin Vine, featured in this photograph of 1976, was still using the old-fashioned brush and rods of the kind with which his family had been cleaning chimneys since 1850. They are still in business in Richmond.

HORNBY'S DAIRY YARD was on the site of the open car park by Richmond station. From here the carts set out with churns from which the milk would be dispensed to householders' own jugs.

SECRETTS DAIRY AT HAM was taken over by Hornby and Clarke in October 1957. This is the last delivery.

MILK DELIVERY in the First World War, outside Richmond Theatre. By then the carts were equipped with small cans for individual deliveries.

BREAD DELIVERY. Newens bakery in the Kew Road supplied their roundsmen with tricycle carts.

7

THE KEW VISCOSE SPINNING SYNDICATE established its works in South Avenue, Kew, in 1893, and it was here that the synthetic fibre then called 'artificial silk' and later 'rayon' was first developed for commercial use, after a means of spinning it had been invented by Charles Topham. The photograph shows members of the firm at the works, after the successful experiments with the 'Topham's box'. The firm was bought out by Courtaulds in 1904, and production was moved to their works in Coventry. (Photograph by courtesy of Courtaulds PLC)

Serving the Community

A RICHMOND FIRE-ENGINE by Little Green, 1912. From the early eighteenth century Richmond had a volunteer fire brigade with manual engines. After the great Star and Garter fire in 1870 the brigade was reorganized on a more regular basis. The first steam engine was acquired in 1875 and a second in 1881. An engine with a fire escape ladder was bought in 1891.

THE RICHMOND VOLUNTEER FIRE BRIGADE outside the station, with their two 'steamers' in the 1880s. Captain T. Covell, the Fire Brigade chief, is on the far right.

THE KEW PALACE FIRE BRIGADE with an old manual engine supplied for use at the palace in George III's reign.

Left:

THE FIRE STATION in the Square, Richmond, 1897. When built in 1870, there was a chute by the clock-tower for the crewmen (see photograph on p. 25). This was removed when the mortuary chapel was built adjoining the tower.

Below:

THE RICHMOND POLICE STATION was transferred about 1890 from its original location in Prince's Street to the new building in George Street seen here on the right. It was moved again, to the present site in Red Lion Street, in 1912. The George Street building was converted into shops.

THE RICHMOND POST OFFICE, C. 1870. Richmond's first post office was in a shop in King Street. From 1843 to 1858 it was at the premises of Lloyd's, chemists, in George Street; but was then moved to Brooks' grocery store at No. 79 George Street (now part of Dickins and Jones). When John Brooks died in 1867 his widow became postmistress. In 1872 she closed the grocery business, and the premises became a post office only. The post office moved to a purpose-built building at No. 70 George Street in 1886, but Mrs Brooks remained postmistress until 1892, when she was succeeded by her son.

THE PETERSHAM POST OFFICE, 1902. Petersham post office was tiny, but independent of Richmond. From the 1850s (and perhaps earlier) it was in charge of successive members of the Long family, who also traded as grocers and then stationers. (T.C. Long was postmaster in 1902.) This wooden building, attached to Ivy House in the Petersham Road, continued to serve until 1924 when the post office was moved to the Petersham Stores (p. 77). It then became a shoe repairer's until destroyed by a bomb in 1941. Petersham finally lost its own post office in 1966.

LAYING THE INTERCEPTING STORM WATER SEWER ON RICHMOND GREEN, 1886. The construction of sewers was one of the many public works undertaken by the Richmond Vestry. The project engineer, Mr Walter Brooke, AMICE, is the top-hatted figure on the left. Opposite him, also in a top hat, is Mr T.M. Clarke, dentist, of No. 9 The Green, the house with the portico on the right of the picture.

THE OFFICES OF THE RICHMOND GAS COMPANY. In 1846 the Richmond Gas Company was established. It set up its works at the junction of the Lower Mortlake Road and Manor Road. In 1882 these new offices were built at the corner of The Green and Duke Street.

THE LOWER MORTLAKE ROAD AND THE GASWORKS. When the new Twickenham and Chiswick Bridges were built in the 1930s, the Lower Mortlake Road was widened. This provided an excellent view of the gas-holders.

THE RICHMOND BOROUGH BEADLES. The Beadles were parish officials, originally to maintain order in the church. As Vestry responsibilities expanded so did the Beadles' role. In eighteenth-century Richmond they shared supervision of the night watch and the fire brigade with the elected constables. After the Metropolitan Police took over in 1830 the Beadles' duties became mainly ceremonial. These are the Beadles of the three civil parishes united in the Borough of Richmond in 1892: (left to right) Mr William Bennett of Petersham, Mr H. Head of Richmond, and Mr George Viner of Kew. All had special uniforms and carried staffs of office.

SECTION SIXTEEN

Education

RUSSELL BRITISH SCHOOL PETERSHAM

THE RUSSELL BRITISH SCHOOL, PETERSHAM, 'National' schools were run by the Church of England; 'British' schools were non-denominational. The Petersham school was built in 1852 at the expense of Lord John Russell on land at the corner of Petersham Park. Destroyed by bombs in November 1943, it was rebuilt on a new site near the gates of Ham House.

THE VINEYARD BRITISH SCHOOLS, RICHMOND, founded 1858. The Junior School, built by public subscription, was opened in 1867. In 1870 it was split into separate sections for boys and girls, and an infants' school was added in 1883. The old buildings have been adapted for housing since the school was moved to new premises in Friars Stile Road.

ST MARY MAGDALENE NATIONAL SCHOOL, RICHMOND. The first free parochial school in Richmond, attached to the parish church, was established in 1713 at the corner of Brewer's Lane. From 1854 until the 1960s the school occupied the buildings at the Eton Street – Paradise Road corner seen on the right of the upper picture. Below, the fourth class in the boys' school, 1904.

ST ANDREW'S NATIONAL SCHOOL, HAM: the infant class in 1893. The old school building is now St Thomas Aquinas' Roman Catholic church.

WEST HEATH SCHOOL, HAM. The Richmond area abounded in private schools. John Minter Morgan, former owner of West Heath House, had promoted the ideals of Pestalozzi in education and of Robert Owen in community living. When West Heath School moved to Sevenoaks, the house became the Cassel Hospital.

COUNTY SCHOOL FOR GIRLS, PARKSHOT, RICHMOND.

THE COUNTY SECONDARY SCHOOL FOR GIRLS, PARKSHOT was built in 1908–9 to rehouse the renamed Richmond High School. In 1974 the pupils were transferred to Shene School, and the building is now the Richmond Adult College.

County School, Richmond.

W8830

THE BOYS' COUNTY SCHOOL, KEW ROAD, opened in 1896. The school hall (on the right) was added later. In 1939 it became a Technical Institute, and later an Institute of Further Education and the Adult College. It is now adapted for housing.

THE RICHMOND PUBLIC LIBRARY, opened in 1881, was one of the first free public libraries in the London area. Above, coronation decorations in 1953. Below, the interior of the library in 1884.

Health and Welfare

THE OPENING OF THE STAR AND GARTER HOME, 10 July 1924. Designed by Edwin Cooper, the new building of the Star and Garter Home for disabled servicemen replaced the Star and Garter Hotel in which the Home was first established during the First World War. The photograph shows the mayor, Councillor W.C. Robinson, presenting an address to King George V. Queen Mary is on the right.

THE ROYAL HOSPITAL, KEW FOOT ROAD, RICHMOND. The Richmond Infirmary was opened in February 1868 in the former home of the Earl of Shaftesbury (and a century earlier of James Thomson, the poet). Queen Victoria became patron in 1895.

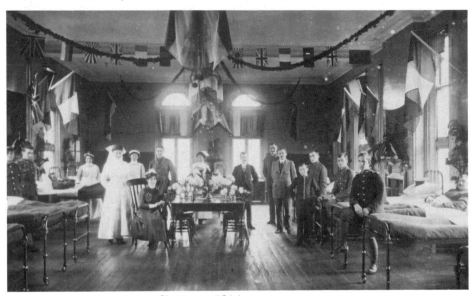

A WARD IN THE ROYAL HOSPITAL, Christmas 1914.

Left:
DUPPA'S ALMSHOUSES in the Vineyard. Richmond had six almshouse foundations, Petersham one and Ham two. Richmond's second foundation, by Brian Duppa, Bishop of Winchester, in 1661, was originally on the Hill but moved to the Vineyard in 1852. The old gateway was moved to the new site.

THE CHURCH ESTATE ALMSHOUSES in the Sheen Road, built in 1844, were one of the two nineteenth-century foundations.

THE RICHMOND WORKHOUSE was built at the expense of King George III in 1786. The clock and cupola were a gift from two local magistrates in 1819. The workhouse building was converted into flats in 1986.

CELLS FOR THE CASUAL POOR, who earned their lodging by breaking stones into pieces small enough to pass through the grilles.

Military and Wartime

CASTLE GATE, Lower Mortlake Road. The headquarters of the 1st Royal Surrey Militia were built in 1856, with a quadrangle of buildings around a parade ground. This photograph was taken in April 1909 by F.A. Turner, just before the demolition of the buildings. The militia headquarters had been moved to 'The Keep' in Kingston about 1870, but for a while the Castlegate building was used for housing poor families. The site was redeveloped in the 1920s, including a road that bears the old name.

OUR VOLUNTEERS:

MEMBERS OF THE RICHMOND DETACHMENT OF THE 3RD VOLUNTEER BATTALION, EAST SURREY REGIMENT, 1899. The Volunteers originally wore riflemen's busbies, but some are wearing forage caps of the type worn by the army in the Second World War.

CARLO, THE COLLECTING DOG, by the old cannon on Richmond Little Green after the outbreak of war in 1914.

THE LONDON SCOTTISH REGIMENT marching into a tented camp in Richmond Park in May 1915.

THE GROVE ROAD HOSPITAL in 1915. The infirmary attached to the Richmond Workhouse, which had been built in 1902, was used as a military hospital in the First World War.

SECOND WORLD WAR BOMBING. The photograph above shows the cottages at 330–32 Kew Road. The one below shows the Town Hall building, damaged by incendiary bombs on 29 November 1940.

AN ANTI-AIRCRAFT GUN SITE inside the Sheen Gate of Richmond Park in the Second World War. The photograph appeared in *Picture Post* of 13 December 1941 without any indication of locality.

THE RICHMOND HOME GUARD ON PARADE.

RICHMOND'S SPITFIRE. Richmond, like many other towns, raised money to pay for a fighter aircraft. The cost of a Hurricane or Spitfire was reckoned as £5,000.

Celebrations

CHARTER DAY 1890; a scene in the Quadrant, Richmond. Richmond obtained its charter as a Borough on 16 July 1890, and on 23 July the Charter was formally brought to Richmond. As usual, the fire brigade had a prominent place in the procession.

QUEEN VICTORIA'S DIAMOND JUBILEE in 1897 was the occasion of great celebrations. These were planned by the committee seen in the upper photograph: Messrs Capel Smith, Downs and Brooks (the postmaster) standing; Messrs Watney, McDougall and Dimbleby (proprietor of the *Richmond and Twickenham Times*) sitting. The lower photograph shows the Jubilee procession passing along George Street.

ETON STREET DECORATED FOR THE DIAMOND JUBILEE. The buildings of St Mary Magdalene National School can be seen at the top end of the street on the right-hand side.

THE DIAMOND JUBILEE FÊTE in the Old Deer Park.

INDIAN OFFICERS AT THE STAR AND GARTER HOTEL, 1897. Cavalry officers of the forces of the Indian Princes (as well as VCOs from the regular Indian Army) were brought to London to ride in the Jubilee procession of the Queen-Empress. They were accommodated at the Star and Garter Hotel, and are here seen on the steps of the garden terrace, with two of the British officers accompanying them.

Above:
THE PROCLAMATION OF KING EDWARD VII at Richmond Town Hall, 1901. The mayor reads the proclamation from the balcony of the Council Chamber.

Right:
A COTTAGE IN WORPLE WAY DECORATED FOR KING EDWARD VII'S CORONATION, 1902. No. 11 Worple Way was the home of Mr T. Pyke, bath chair proprietor, standing proudly at his gate.

RICHMOND TOWN HALL decorated for King George V's Silver Jubilee in 1935.

THE MAYORAL PROCESSION, 1939, passing the end of Brewer's Lane in George Street.

VANCOUVER DAY CELEBRATIONS, 18 May 1936 There were special celebrations in 1936, when the City of Vancouver in British Columbia was celebrating its Golden Jubilee. The graveside ceremony (see p. 75) was attended by the Secretary of State for the Dominions, Mr Malcolm MacDonald (speaking at the microphone in the upper picture), the Lord Mayor of London and the Mayor of King's Lynn (Vancouver's birthplace). A wreath from the city of Vancouver was placed on the grave. A painting of Petersham churchyard by Mr A. Watson Turnbull (lower picture), was handed to the Lord Mayor to take to Vancouver on his forthcoming visit, as a gift from Richmond.

ACKNOWLEDGEMENTS

Most of the photographs reproduced in this book come from the Local Studies Collection of the Richmond Public Library, and we are grateful to the Council of the London Borough of Richmond upon Thames for permission to use them.

Special thanks are due to Miss Diana Howard, Principal Librarian (Reference and Information Services), and to Miss Jane Baxter, Assistant Librarian in charge of the Local Studies Collection, for their help to the compilers in assembling the photographs selected.

Thanks are also due to John Cloake, Mrs Florence Edmonds, Raymond Gill, Miss Sylvia Greenwood and Miss Sylvia Penn for lending photographs from their private collections to be copied, as also to Newens Bakery and to the Museum of Richmond.

The Fox Talbot photograph on p. 6 is reproduced with permission of the Trustees of the Science Museum (negative no. 232/66); the aerial photograph of Ham on p. 84 is Crown copyright and is reproduced with the permission of the Controller of Her Britannic Majesty's Stationery Office; the group photograph of the Kew Viscose Spinning Syndicate on p. 128 is reproduced with permission of Courtaulds PLC.